EVERYONE A BUTTERFLY

Forty Sermons for Children

RANDY HAMMER

SKINNER HOUSE BOOKS
BOSTON

This book is dedicated to the many children, including my own son and daughter, with whom I have had the privilege and pleasure of sharing Children's Time.

Printed in the United States.

Text and cover design by Suzanne Morgan.

ISBN 1-55896-480-0
978-1-55896-480-8

Library of Congress Cataloging-in-Publication Data

Hammer, Randy, 1955-
   Everyone a butterfly : forty sermons for children / Randy
Hammer.
      p. cm.
   ISBN 1-55896-480-0 (alk. paper)
1. Children's sermons. I. Title.

BV4315.H278 2004
252'.53—dc22

                                                    2004014927

6 5 4 3 2
12 11 10 09

CONTENTS

INTRODUCTION

After more than a quarter century in full-time parish ministry, I can say with certainty that one of the most challenging aspects of pastoral leadership is planning the part of the Sunday service that's for the children—variously called Children's Time, Time with the Children, Children's Message, Children's Sermon, Children's Parable, or as it is in my current parish, The Young Church. Many Saturday evenings have found me frantically trying to find or prepare a children's message for the following morning's service.

The aim of this book is to offer quality children's sermons for progressive clergy and congregations. Although there are a number of published collections of sermons for children, most of them present a theological perspective that differs from my own. One will not find in this collection, for instance, messages that seek to focus young listeners on their sinful natures or to elevate the followers of one faith tradition over those of another. I identify as a liberal Christian Universalist, but I hope this book will prove to be helpful for a wide audience as each of these sermons focuses on the general theme of the inherent worth and dignity of all people. Sophia Lyon Fahs, that pioneer in religious education, writes, "One of the most important of man's beliefs is what he thinks about himself." At the heart of each of these sermons is the idea that each child is loved and wanted, each child is valuable—to his or her friends and family, and to his or her community of faith. As Jerry Marshall Jordan reminds us, we must "strive to instill a sense of self-worth in our children. The mere fact that we take the time in the worship service to sit with them in that big sanctuary with all the adults present means more than words can fully express. . . . And it is not just what is *done* to teach this self-esteem, but also what is said, reminding them that they are created in the 'image of God.'"

The sermons in this collection are based on some underlying assumptions and guidelines, which I offer you now:

~ A quality children's sermon is not condescending, and therefore one children's sermon does not fit all. You need to know the children—their ages, levels of maturity, and individual personalities. Presenting a parable suitable for three-year-olds to a group of ten-year-olds wastes an opportunity to reach out to them. Begin with where children are and seek to answer the questions children are asking.

~ A good sermon is concerned with universal truth and universal human need. Children have an emotional need to feel their relationship to the larger world they are discovering. In the words of Joseph Campbell, "We need myths that will identify the individual not with his local group but with the planet."

~ Your sermon should spark the children's imagination. As Bruno Bettelheim reminds us, "For a story truly to hold the child's attention, it must entertain him and arouse his curiosity. But to enrich his life, it must stimulate his imagination." Bettelheim warns against stories that "peg the child's imagination to the level he has already reached on his own." Our aim should be to invite the child's soul to see at greater depths. Children should be encouraged to be and do more than they are now doing, to stretch themselves to their full potential. One way to do this is to encourage young listeners to participate in the development of the story or subject.

~ A good sermon nourishes self-understanding. Listeners should be invited to discover their unique identities and to deal with inner conflicts.

~ Children's sermons should enable children to relate positively to the world around them. As Fahs reminds us, we are all one with the natural world and "the material of the earth and stars" is in us.

~ Sermons for children should be simple, centered around a single truth. As Jordan says, "The use of an object should remind the children of something, and then lead into a simple truth that can be internalized with their own experiential under-standing." He also notes, "Some experiences are so profound in and of themselves (such as birth, death, suffering, disappointment, as well as won-der, joy, hope, love) that the ultimate questions arising from them require some profound answers simply stated."

~ Be sure to speak to all ages in your audience, chil-dren and adults alike. Though a good children's message is presented in a way that a child can grasp, it will also, like the great nursery rhymes, sustain the interest of and be meaningful to adults. But a word of caution is in order. The children's sermon should never be used in an indirect way to preach to the adults under the guise of something for the children. The children's special moment in the service is not the time to deliver messages that are over their heads or don't concern them.

~ The children's sermon is not a time to get a laugh at the children's expense. Don't take the Art Linkletter approach by asking the children a ques-tion that will elicit funny answers for the benefit of the adults. This is a sacred time, in which the dig-nity of all congregants, old and young, should be respected and affirmed.

~ Appeal to as many of the senses as possible. Sight, touch, taste, and smell are as important as the words you say.

~ Watch the length. Seven to eight minutes is a good length to shoot for. A good children's sermon should be long enough to be meaningful but considerate of the young audience's attention span.

~ Your sermon should be told and not read. Bettelheim says, "The telling of the story to a child, to be most effective, has to be an interpersonal event, shaped by those who participate in it."

~ If possible, your sermon should support the readings, topic, or sermon of the day.

~ Use inclusive language. To some extent, this involves personal choice. Since I believe that God is neither male nor female, I try not to refer to God with the masculine pronouns. Neither am I comfortable referring to God as "She." I strive to phrase my sentences in such a way that the use of a pronoun for God is unnecessary. Language is a powerful teacher, even when we don't intend it to be. Try to avoid referring to one gender more than the other. Include a broad variety of children's names and set aside stereotypical preconceptions, such as the notion that doctors are male and flight attendants are female.

The children we serve, created in the divine image, deserve the very best that we have to offer. The children's time in the worship service offers you a meaningful opportunity to reach out and speak directly to those in your faith community who are frequently looked over and spoken down to. By the care and imagination that you invest in your words to them, you can teach them that they are valued members of your church.

These forty sermons are drawn from biblical literature, classic children's literature, ordinary observations, and historical documents. One of the primary sources of inspiration here is nature itself—our greatest teacher and a natural subject for children. I have included suggestions for presenting the sermons and adapting them to your own needs, as well as follow-up activities to help listeners process and internalize the message. For each sermon, I have suggested an object or picture that you can use to help the children connect to the story visually. It is a good idea to keep the object for sharing concealed in a "mystery" bag or box until the appropriate time. In offering this collection, it is my hope that these sermons will not only free up your Saturday nights but also get your creative juices flowing.

EVERYONE A BUTTERFLY

All people are beautiful in their own way.

The story of the Monarch butterfly is one of life's greatest mysteries and miracles. Every year, the Monarchs migrate south to places like the mountains in central Mexico, and then in a few months they migrate back north again. The longest distance that the Monarch butterflies are known to travel is from Ontario, Canada, to central Mexico, a distance of about 1,800 miles! The butterfly is one of earth's most beautiful and graceful creatures, and the Monarch butterfly is the prettiest of them all. It has bright reddish-brown wings with white dots and a black border.

But the Monarch butterfly was not always so beautiful. Before it becomes the creature that you and I picture when we think of butterflies, it goes through several stages. First it is an egg, laid by its mother. Eventually it becomes a caterpillar and then it hibernates inside a cocoon until finally it reaches adulthood and emerges as a colorful butterfly. This process of change is called *metamorphosis*. The creature that eventually becomes the Monarch butterfly is not always beautiful, but the potential to become beautiful is always there inside, just waiting to get out.

We have a lot in common with the butterfly. Sometimes we can let ourselves say and do things that aren't very beautiful, things that show us at our worst instead of our best, things that can bring hurt to ourselves and to those around us. But each of us has the potential for great beauty. That beauty was given to us when we were created.

The butterfly has long been a religious symbol that reminds us of the new life and positive change that is possible for all of us. So, whenever you see a butterfly, may it be a reminder of the beauty that is within each of us, the beauty that is just waiting to get out and bring a blessing to the world.

OBJECT FOR SHARING: A picture of a Monarch butterfly or a live butterfly that you lovingly keep in a safe container and then release.

SUGGESTIONS FOR PRESENTATION: This story will work best in the spring or early summer, perhaps most effectively on Easter Sunday. Props such as binoculars and a butterfly net would add interest and intrigue to the story.

FOLLOW-UP ACTIVITIES: Encourage the children to do further research on butterflies or to research the butterfly's presence in religious artwork.

TREASURES FROM THE SEA

All homes are different—and special.

Good morning, everyone! As you can see, I have brought a treasure chest with me this morning. And my treasure chest is full of treasures from the sea. Would anyone like to guess what kinds of sea treasures are in the chest? [*Some will probably guess seashells.*]

That is correct—I have a treasure chest full of seashells. I am going to let each of you select one shell from the chest, and then we will talk about them. [*Allow time for each child to reach into the chest and select a shell.*]

As you look at the different shells that you have chosen, what do you notice? All of them are different in some way. No two shells are exactly alike. Notice the different shapes, sizes, colors, and texture. What colors do you see in the shells? Feel your shell. Is it smooth or rough?

4

Can anyone tell us what these shells were originally? They were homes to different kinds of sea creatures. Inside these shells, real, live creatures of the sea used to live.

You know, that is the thing about homes, isn't it? All homes are different—not only with creatures of the sea, but with humans as well. All of us here today come from different homes. And no two of those homes are exactly alike. Some live in big homes, and some live in small homes. Some live in brick homes, and some live in wooden homes. Some live in homes that are white on the outside, and some live in homes that are another color.

But the families who live inside our homes are different as well. No two families are exactly alike. Some homes have a mom and dad and two daughters. Some have a mom and dad and two sons. Some have a dad and daughter, and others have a mom and a son. Some homes have two moms, and some have two dads.

The fact that our homes are all different doesn't make one home better than another one. They're just different, that's all.

So if you meet someone here at church, at school, or at some sports outing whose family is different from yours, remember the lesson of the seashells—all homes may be different, but each and every one is special and has special people living in it, like you.

———

OBJECT FOR SHARING: A variety of seashells.

SUGGESTIONS FOR PRESENTATION: This lesson will work best in late summer or early fall, when summer vacation is still fresh in everyone's mind. If possible, secure some form of small treasure chest to hold the shells. Some stores sell these during the winter holidays as gift-wrap boxes. Or, with a bit of imagination, a treasure chest could be crafted for this and future children's stories. You may choose to give each child a shell at the conclusion of the lesson. However, it may be best to let each child choose a shell near the beginning of the lesson; otherwise, the children may be distracted and tempted to reach inside the treasure chest during the lesson itself.

FOLLOW-UP ACTIVITIES: Lead the children in creating a natural home for earth's creatures by using the shells to decorate a fish tank or to help create a terrarium.

MIGHTY OAKS

Each child has the potential for greatness.

Good morning, everyone! I have brought something with me this morning, and you are not going to believe me when I tell you what it is. Would anyone like to venture a guess?

Well, those are all good guesses, but none of them is correct. Actually, I am holding in my hand a mighty oak tree. [*"No's," smiles, and shaking of heads may follow.*] Well, maybe I should say I am holding in my hand the potential for a mighty oak tree. Anybody want to guess again what I am holding in my hand? [*Perhaps someone will now guess an acorn.*]

That's right, I am holding an acorn. You see, acorns like this one grow on mighty oak trees. And when an acorn falls to the ground in just the right spot and at just the right time, it can sprout and become a tiny oak seedling that may eventually grow up to be a mighty oak tree.

So what I am holding is the possibility for a mighty oak tree. It takes a long time for a mighty oak tree to grow tall. Some are as old as one hundred years. But the oak tree has to start somewhere, and it starts with a tiny acorn just like this one.

You know, it is sort of that way with each of you. Inside each of you is something called potential. And what is potential? Potential is possibility. When each of us was created, the possibility for greatness was put inside us. If we are able to discover the wonderful potential that is within and nurture it, each of us may grow up to do something important and special. One of the aims of the religious education here at our church is to help each of you to find and develop the greatness within.

We won't grow up to be mighty oak trees, will we? But we can grow up to be special in many other ways.

OBJECT FOR SHARING: An acorn.

SUGGESTIONS FOR PRESENTATION: The fall is a good time for this children's message because acorns are available and because most churches are kicking off the new religious education year. Gather enough acorns so that every child may take one at the close of the children's message.

FOLLOW-UP ACTIVITIES: You can make use of the acorns later as a craft activity by having the children glue them to name tags, which might read: "My Name Is _____. I'm a Mighty Oak in the Making," or, "I am full of potential." Or drill tiny holes through the acorns and have the children thread string through them to make bracelets.

WATER WORLD

We are all connected.

You know, there is nothing in the world better than a cold glass of water on a hot summer day. Sometimes we forget just how important water is to us until we go for a long time without having any and get really thirsty. Water is one of those blessings of life that, if we are not careful, we can easily take for granted.

Water is a funny thing. It falls from the sky in the form of rain, snow, or dew. It soaks into the ground and runs into underground springs or into creeks, rivers, lakes, and oceans. We drink some of the water, but much of it evaporates up to the clouds, where it comes down as rain, snow, or dew again.

Scientists tell us that our bodies are actually from 50 to 75 percent water. Where do you think most of the water in our bodies is found? That's right, in our blood. Then, when we grow old and die, the water in our bodies goes back into the earth to be recycled again.

Some congregations have a practice that they call *water communion*. At the beginning of the new church year, after everyone has returned from summer vacations, people bring some water from their travels and everyone pours his or her water into a big bowl, where it is mixed together. This reminds us that the life of everyone is connected with all of creation.

Great men and women who lived long ago drank water just as we do. The water they drank went back into the earth to be recycled. So today, when we drink water, we might be drinking the same water that Moses, Joan of Arc, Buddha, or Jesus drank. What was once in Moses, Joan of Arc, Buddha, and Jesus could now be in us. Isn't that an exciting thought!

But that is really what we believe anyway, isn't it? That the goodness and greatness that was in all the great men and women of the past can also be in us!

OBJECT FOR SHARING: A glass of water. If you can, bring water from some point of interest like Niagara Falls.

SUGGESTIONS FOR PRESENTATION: This message will work best in September, when everyone has returned from vacation. If you can plan months in advance, ask the children in May and remind them in summer newsletters to bring water from their summer travels to be included in this Children's Time in September.

FOLLOW-UP ACTIVITIES: Children might like to research the mention of water in the Scriptures, especially the first chapter of Genesis. Encourage the children to think of ways that water may be better appreciated and protected as a natural resource. Finally, you might use the water gathered for water communion to plant a tree, perhaps on a Sunday near Arbor Day.

A BOX OF CRAYONS

Though we are all different, we must live together.

Good morning, girls and boys. How many of you like crayons? I like crayons, too. When I was your age, one of the most exciting things about going back to school in the fall was getting a brand-new box of crayons, just like this one. [*Hold a new box of 48 or 64 crayons for all to see.*] It was nice that each and every one was fresh and sharp. I even liked the way that they smelled. Would you like to smell? [*Take a moment to pass the box under the noses of those who show interest.*]

You know, we can learn a lot from a box of crayons. One thing we notice is that every one of them is a different color. There are no two crayons in this box exactly alike. You might have a favorite color of crayon that is not my favorite color at all. And I may have a favorite color that you don't like at all. And wouldn't it be sad if all the crayons in a box were the exact same color? That would be pretty dull, wouldn't it? Every color is important and needed. And each crayon has a different name. Some of them even have unfamiliar-sounding names, like *fuchsia*. Others have common names, like *blue*. As the crayons are used a lot, some of them get dull. Others may become weak and even broken.

But even though we may think that some crayons are prettier than others and some are weak and broken, all of them are important and all have to live in the same box.

Isn't that the way it is with us, as God's children? Our skin colors may be different. Some of us may think that we are not as pretty as others we know. Some of us may not be as strong or healthy as others. And some of us may not like our names.

Nevertheless, each one of us—and every other child we know and meet—is important, and all of us have to live on the same earth. That means we all need to learn to get along and respect and care for one another. And that includes those who may be different from us.

We all have to live in the same box, just like the crayons.

———————

OBJECT FOR SHARING: A new box of 48 or 64 crayons.

SUGGESTIONS FOR PRESENTATION: This lesson would work well in the early fall, when children are starting back to school. Give each child a small box (eight or so) of crayons to take to religious education class or to take home as a reminder of the story.

FOLLOW-UP ACTIVITIES: Invite the children to draw children of different skin colors. Encouraging them to think of and write as many different children's names as possible, being respectful of each name mentioned, would also reinforce the lesson.

A NEW LEAF

We all have the power to change.

What is this? [*Wait for someone to say "a leaf."*] Of course it is. That was easy, wasn't it? [*Then take another leaf and hold it up.*] Now, what is this? It is a new leaf. [*Turn the leaf upside down a number of times.*] Does anyone know what that is? It is turning over a new leaf.

Perhaps that is a phrase you have heard before—*turning over a new leaf.* Does anyone know what it means?

Turning over a new leaf is an old saying that means to have a new beginning, to make a change, or to start fresh. In the Bible, a man by the name of Paul speaks about walking "in the newness of life," (Romans 6:4). For instance, someone who hasn't been living in a very nice way may decide to change and start living in a nicer, more loving, more compassionate way. Someone who has never attended church services might decide to start attending church regularly. Can you think of other ways that one might turn over a new leaf?

One of the great things about us is that we have been created with the power of choice. That is, we are free to choose. All of us can choose how we are going to live and what we are going to do with our lives.

And every now and again, all of us need to decide that we are going to make a change in our lives, start afresh, have a new beginning. Each of us has the option of "turning over a new leaf."

OBJECT FOR SHARING: Enough leaves so that each child can have one.

SUGGESTIONS FOR PRESENTATION: This lesson will work best in the fall, when the leaves have turned and are just beginning to fall. You can use large boughs of fall leaves to decorate the sanctuary in lieu of flowers.

FOLLOW-UP ACTIVITIES: Show the children how to place leaves under a sheet of paper and color over them with crayons to create a rubbing of the leaf. If a laminating machine is available, the children could place the leaves on wide strips of construction paper and then laminate them in clear plastic to make bookmarks or place mats.

BRINGING BUCKETS TO CHURCH

All people have something to offer.

Good morning! I brought my bucket to church today. I bet that if buckets could talk, some of them would tell some wonderful stories about good times they have had in the sand or by the shore, but very few would tell us about coming to church.

We don't usually bring our buckets to church, do we? But if we did bring our buckets to church every Sunday, I wonder if we would bring something in them, or if we would bring them empty so that we could take something home.

Let's use our imaginations and pretend for a minute. You want to? Let's suppose that we decided to bring our buckets to church every Sunday. What do you suppose we might bring in them? Those are some fine answers.

But let's suppose that we could reach deep down inside of us and pull out those gifts that each of us has been given and that we could put them in the bucket. How about the gift of singing? How about we pretend that we are going to put *that* in our bucket to bring to church? And how about the gift of drawing? How about we pretend to put *that* in our bucket to bring to church? And how about the gift of friendliness, and the ability to smile and make others happy, and the ability to be a helper around the church building? How about we pretend to put *all* of those things in our bucket to bring them to church?

Now, what do you do with a bucket when it is full? That's right—you pour it out. And where might we pour out everything we have pretended to put in our buckets? How about on the altar or place where we put our gifts, as a gift to God?

An important thing for us to remember is that every one of us has gifts inside that we can share. A man by the name of Peter wrote in the Bible, "Serve one another with whatever gift each of you has received" (1 Peter 4:10). We may not be able to carry our gifts in a bucket, but they are there inside all of us, and all of them are important.

OBJECT FOR SHARING: A children's sand bucket.

SUGGESTIONS FOR PRESENTATION: This story will work well during the congregation's fall stewardship campaign. The Sunday prior to this presentation, ask the children to bring their sand buckets to church the following Sunday. Then secure enough extras to share them with children who don't remember to bring one.

FOLLOW-UP ACTIVITIES: Encourage the children to make a list of all the gifts they have to share.

A FRIEND AT SCHOOL

Everyone can be a good friend.

Today I want to tell you a story about my friend Kara. Her day hadn't started out very well. Kara had overslept. She had time to eat only half of her breakfast. She had forgotten to do some of her homework. And it was pouring down rain.

Kara's dad dropped her off at the school door. As she was running toward the building to get out of the rain, she tripped and fell down in the mud. Notebooks and lunch bag and pencils and crayons flew everywhere. Kara was so embarrassed.

About that time, along came Kyle. *Kyle*, Kara thought, *is the teacher's pet. He always gets out of class to run errands.* Kara said, "Can you help me, please?" But Kyle just yelled, "I'm running an errand for Miss Holloway. Tough luck, Kara." Then he ran into the building.

Kara tried to get up, but she slipped in the mud and fell back down again just as Sonja walked up beside her. *Sonja will help me*, Kara thought. The principal asked Sonja to be hall monitor at least once a week. Sonja reached out her hand as though she were going to help Kara up. But as Kara reached up towards Sonja, Sonja jerked her hand away and began laughing. "Look at Kruddy Kara! Look at Kruddy Kara!" she yelled, calling attention to Kara lying there in the mud. Everyone turned to look and laugh at Kara. She started to cry.

But then along came Brian, a new boy in school. "Oh, he'll never help me," Kara murmured to herself. "He doesn't even know me."

But Brian knelt down beside Kara there in the mud and began to pick up her things. "Can I help you up?" Brian asked as he stuck his hand out to her. For a second, Kara didn't know what to think. But then she took Brian's hand, and he helped her back to her feet. He carried all her things inside for her and then said, "I'll hold your things and wait for you in the hall while you go to the bathroom and clean up." Kara nodded okay.

When she returned, Brian was still standing there waiting for her. "Thank you for helping me," Kara said, a little embarrassed.

"Ah, it's nothing," Brian replied. "Anybody can be a friend." Brian handed Kara her things and then turned to go to his classroom. Kara smiled a big smile. The day didn't seem so bad after all.

OBJECT FOR SHARING: A child's book bag containing paper, pencils, crayons, and other school supplies.

SUGGESTIONS FOR PRESENTATION: Since this story is based on the biblical story of the Good Samaritan (Luke 10:30-37), you might want to use this story on a Sunday when the biblical passage is used either in religious education class or worship. Consider holding an umbrella or wearing a yellow slicker and rubber boots while you tell this story.

FOLLOW-UP ACTIVITIES: Encourage the children to think of other scenarios in which they could prove to be a friend to others in need.

SMALL GIFTS

It's not the size of the gift that matters.

Who knows what is the smallest coin in U.S. money? That's right—it's the penny. How many pennies does it take to make a dollar? That's right—it takes one hundred. A penny won't buy much these days. Back in the old days, when some of us were your age, you could buy a piece of bubble gum or one piece of hard candy with a penny. But you can't even do that these days.

One day, Jesus and his disciples were in the Temple. And they were watching as people walked by and put their offerings in the collection box. A poor old woman dropped in two tiny copper coins, worth less than one penny. Well, Jesus was happy with the woman. He said, "Look at her; she has done well." Why did Jesus say that? Because the poor woman didn't have much to give, but she gave the best that she had.

Sometimes we may think that we don't have much to offer God or the church. As we look at others who are bigger and have a lot of talent and a lot of money, we may feel small. We may feel like we don't have much to give.

But the important thing is that we give the best we have to give. When we sing, we can sing our best. When we help out around the church by straightening up chairs or straightening up the pews, we can do our best. When we learn in religious education class, we can learn the best that we can learn. And when we give an offering, we can give the best that we have to give.

And when we give our very best, we can be very happy with what we give, even though we may think our gift is very small.

————————

OBJECT FOR SHARING: Small coins, perhaps from different countries.

SUGGESTIONS FOR PRESENTATION: Drop the coins in a collection box or plate so that the children hear as well as see the message. If someone in the congregation is dramatically inclined, he or she could dress up as an elderly widow and come to the front and drop the coins in the collection to reinforce the story.

FOLLOW-UP ACTIVITIES: The children could help count and roll the pennies of the daily offering while continuing to discuss the story.

IMPROVING THE CHURCH

Each of us can help make things better.

Who can tell us what day is coming up this week? That's right—Halloween. Some interesting things have happened on Halloween in years past. This morning I would like to share with you something that happened on Halloween a long, long time ago.

About five hundred years ago, there was a priest whose name was Martin Luther. This young priest looked at the church of his day and saw a lot of things that needed to be improved or made better. So he sat down and wrote out ninety-five things—he called them *theses*—that he felt were wrong with the church and needed to be changed. The story goes that on October 31, 1517, young man Luther took a hammer and nail and nailed his ninety-five statements to the door of the village church. What he was hoping for was that the other ministers would sit down with him and talk about how they could make the church better.

Well, as you might imagine, people did not like what Luther did. He was arrested and held in a castle. He was told to take back the things he had said about the church. But Luther said, "I can't do that." So the authorities continued to hold him in the castle. But you know what? Luther used that time to accomplish something very good. He began to translate the Bible from the Latin into German so his people could read the Bible in their own language.

Well, eventually, Martin Luther was released. But by nailing his ninety-five theses to the church door, he started what we know as the Protestant Reformation. Those who took part in the Protestant Reformation were protesting about what they thought was wrong with the church, and they were trying to make it better. Our congregation and the denomination to which we belong trace our beginnings back to the Protestant Reformation that started with Luther.

We certainly don't want anybody driving nails in the beautiful doors of our church, do we? But all of us are called to do what we can to make our church and our world better.

OBJECT FOR SHARING: A hammer, nail, and parchment paper with "theses" printed on it.

SUGGESTIONS FOR PRESENTATION: Bring a board to church on which to nail the "theses" at the beginning of the lesson, reinforcing the audible aspect of learning. Work with the music director to include Luther's hymn "A Mighty Fortress Is Our God" in the worship service and explain its significance to the Reformation movement.

FOLLOW-UP ACTIVITIES: Encourage the children to write their own "theses" of how their church could be improved.

A LITTLE SQUIRRELLY

Don't give up.

Do you like birdfeeders? I love birdfeeders. I enjoy watching the birds scurry for food, especially on a cold, snowy winter day. Do you know who else likes birdfeeders? Squirrels. Squirrels love birdfeeders even more than we humans do. Why do squirrels love birdfeeders? That's right—because of the birdseed that they find there. Anyone who has squirrels around knows that it is almost impossible to keep food in a birdfeeder for the birds. The squirrels tend to eat it all. But squirrels are earth's creatures, too, so I guess that's all right.

Many people who study animals think that squirrels are one of the ten smartest animals in the world. That makes them pretty smart, considering how many different types of animals there are in the world. It doesn't matter where you hang a birdfeeder or how you hang it, sooner or later the squirrels will probably figure out a way to get to it.

You see, even though they are small, squirrels use the brain that God gave them to figure out a way to solve the problems that get in their way. Squirrels have what is called *tenacity*. Does anyone know what tenacity means? To be tenacious or to have tenacity means to be stubborn in not letting yourself be defeated. It means not giving up.

So, are you squirrelly? Perhaps you have heard of someone being called a little bit "squirrelly." What that means is the person is seen to be a little odd or nutty. But being "squirrelly" can be a good thing—if, like the squirrels, we put to good use the brains that we were given to solve the problems that often get in our way, and if, like the squirrels, we are tenacious in problem-solving and don't give up.

———————

OBJECT FOR SHARING: A small birdfeeder with a small amount of birdseed. A stuffed squirrel attached to the side would add a little humor.

SUGGESTIONS FOR PRESENTATION: This lesson will work well on Earth Day or a Sunday when the focus is on ecology or environmental concerns.

FOLLOW-UP ACTIVITIES: Have the children assist in filling birdfeeders with birdseed or making feeders from pine cones and peanut butter sprinkled with birdseed (reinforcing the lesson with touch). Then help the children hang the birdfeeders on the church lawn. Or, if time and resources permit, teach the children to make some simple birdfeeders that they can take home.

BOBBY BOUNCES BACK

Do the right thing.

One day, Bobby came through the house bouncing a new ball.

"Bobby, where did you get your new ball?" his mother asked him.

Bobby hesitated. "Uh, uh, I got it at the pharmacy on my way home from school."

"How much did it cost?" was his mother's next question.

Again, Bobby didn't know how to answer. "Uh, uh, it cost five dollars. Yes, that's right, it cost five dollars."

"Bobby, five dollars seems like quite a lot for a ball like that," his mother said, beginning to sound suspicious.

Tears began to trickle down Bobby's face. "I, I took it when no one was looking," he confessed.

"Bobby! I'm surprised at you," his mother said. "That's stealing. You know we taught you to never take something that doesn't belong to you."

"I know," Bobby moaned, "but when I saw the ball I wanted it so much that I couldn't help it. So I stuffed it in my coat and ran out of the store when no one was looking."

"Bobby, I must confess that I am very disappointed in your behavior," his mother said sadly.

"But no one will ever know," Bobby protested. "No one saw me."

"That's where you are wrong, Bobby," his mother disagreed. "I will know, and most importantly, you will always know. Every time you bounce that ball, you are going to be reminded of how you got it and be reminded that what you did was wrong. I hope you will think about that."

Bobby went to his room to think. After dinner, he went to bed early. But he had a hard time going to sleep. He could not forget what his mother had said.

The next day was Saturday. Bobby got up early. The first thing he did was open the drawer where he kept his allowance and take out six dollars. As soon as he finished breakfast, he ran down the street to the pharmacy where he had taken the ball. Bobby was nervous and breathing hard. He almost didn't go in. But finally he got up the courage to open the door and walk up to the cash register.

"Yes, may I help you?" the clerk said, looking down at Bobby and smiling.

"Uh, I was in here yesterday, and, and …"

"Yes, go on," the clerk said.

"I was in here yesterday and I, I took a ball from right over there" (Bobby pointed to where he had found the ball) "and I took it without paying for it." Bobby plopped the money down on the counter.

The clerk studied him for a moment and then said, "You are a very brave young man for coming in here and doing the right thing. Your parents should be proud of you." The clerk got one of the balls from the shelf and scanned it for the price. "That will be three dollars," the clerk said. "You get to take three dollars back."

Bobby left the store feeling like a big weight had been lifted off of him. He was glad that soon his mother would know he had done the right thing. And most importantly, Bobby himself would always know that he had done what was right.

———————

OBJECT FOR SHARING: A rubber ball.

SUGGESTIONS FOR PRESENTATION: For churches that follow the Christian Lectionary and Church Year, this story works well during Lent, when the temptation of Jesus is the theme of the day. To reinforce the story visually and audibly, bounce the ball as the children gather.

FOLLOW-UP ACTIVITIES: Ask the children to think of a time when they did something wrong but later made it right. Invite them to share how this experience made them feel.

EAGLES IN FLIGHT

Reach for the clouds.

Good morning, everyone! This morning, I would like to invite you to use your imaginations and pretend that instead of a girl or boy, you are a bird. If you could be any bird that you wanted to be, which one would it be? Would anyone like to share with the rest of us which bird you would like to be? [*Give the children time to name the types of bird they would like to be. There probably will not be time for children to tell why they chose the bird they did. And no child should be embarrassed for not wanting to respond.*] Those are all good answers.

You know, some people might choose the eagle. The eagle has long been noted for its keen vision and its strength in flight, as well as its speed, courage, and power, which allow it to fly high above the earth. In the Bible, the eagle is often symbolic of God's care for us. It is not surprising that the eagle became a national emblem for ancient Persia and Rome. The eagle is still found today on some American coins.

Many Native Americans hold the eagle to be sacred, a symbol of the Great Spirit who fills the entire universe.

I bet the eagle is the bird that Isaiah, the Hebrew prophet, would have chosen to be. Isaiah speaks very highly of the eagle in the Bible. "Those who wait for the Lord," Isaiah says, "shall mount up with wings like eagles" (Isaiah 40:31). In other words, those who take time each day to seek the power that comes from God will gain new strength. They will be able to see life more clearly. They will gain much-needed encouragement. And they will be able to fly, like the eagle, higher than they have ever flown before.

So I would like to encourage each of you to set your sights high. As you live your life and plan for the future, be strong, reach for the clouds, and be the very best that you have been created to be.

OBJECT FOR SHARING: A picture or sculpture of an eagle.

SUGGESTIONS FOR PRESENTATION: When noting that "the eagle is still found today on some coins," hold a quarter in the palm of your hand so the children can see the eagle.

FOLLOW-UP ACTIVITIES: Invite the children to explain why they chose the birds that they chose earlier. Encourage the children to name as many different places as possible where they might find images of birds, especially the eagle. If a Native American is a member or friend of the congregation, invite him or her to address the children and go into more detail about the significance of the eagle in Native American thought.

GOD IN A BOX?

There is a bit of the holy in every child.

Good morning! What if I told you that I have God—all of God—in this box? Would you believe me? [*Some of the children will protest.*] Of course you wouldn't. God is much too big to contain in a box, any box.

But a long, long time ago, people thought that they could keep God in a box and carry God with them in that box wherever they went. And as long as God was with them in the box, then things would go well for them. At least that is what they thought. But eventually people began to understand that you can't put God in a box and make God stay there.

But it just may be that there is a *little* part of God in this box—because wherever we see beauty or creation, we see evidence of God. "Only God can make a tree," a poet once said. And this wooden box was once a tree.

But when we look up at the sky at night and see the far-away stars, we know that a part of God is way up there, too. So there is no way to put all of God in a box.

In fact, everywhere we look we see evidence of God's presence. And that means that inside each one of us—inside of me and inside of you—there is a little part of God. "God created man and woman in God's own image," the book of Genesis tells us. Wow! That's an amazing thought, isn't it? To think that there is a little part of God inside of us.

You know what is really exciting? It is to let that piece of God that is inside of us grow and grow so that others see the God part in us.

Someone that comes to mind this morning who really let the God part show in him was Mr. Fred Rogers, of *Mr. Rogers' Neighborhood*. For almost forty years, Mr. Rogers touched the lives of millions of boys and girls because he let the God part that was in him grow and grow and grow so that it showed in his love, compassion, kindness, understanding, and helpfulness.

We should all try, like Mr. Rogers, to let the little part of God within us grow and grow and show itself to everyone we meet.

OBJECT FOR SHARING: A small wooden box or basket with a lid or a larger decorated box with wooden dowel handles attached.

SUGGESTIONS FOR PRESENTATION: This lesson will work well near the Jewish New Year, when covenant renewal is emphasized. Have two people carry the box into the presentation space in a ceremonial way, as the ancient Hebrews carried the Ark of the Covenant.

FOLLOW-UP ACTIVITIES: Encourage the children to draw pictures of or talk about someone who is "letting God show" in his or her life. Discuss ways that members of the congregation let their God part show by participating in outreach and social justice efforts. Secure a big cardboard box so the children can take turns playing "Jack in the box."

FROM COAL TO DIAMONDS

Our problems help make us who we are.

Can anybody tell us what coal is? Coal is a black, rock-like substance that was made millions of years ago deep in the earth. Scientists think that long, long ago, plants such as ferns that grew in swamps died and decomposed. Over time, what was left became this hard mineral substance that we call *coal*. Many people used to use coal to heat their homes in winter because it burns so well and gives off such warm heat.

Coal is made up largely of something called *carbon*. But do you know of another kind of rock that is primarily carbon? It is the diamond. But the difference between the diamond, which is made of carbon, and coal, which is also made of carbon, is that millions of years ago tremendous heat and tremendous pressure turned some carbon deposits into diamonds. In fact, without tremendous heat and tremendous pressure, there can be no diamonds.

Diamonds are one of the hardest and most valuable substances that we know of. Sometimes it is fun to go to the jewelry department in a department store and look at all the diamonds in the window.

You know, sometimes in life we feel pressured. And our parents may feel pressured. We have problems. We worry about things. We have schoolwork to do. We have jobs that we may be expected to do around the house. We may be tempted to do things we know we shouldn't do. We might think of all these things as pressures.

But you know, sometimes pressures can be good for us. Sometimes pressures can make us stronger and wiser. Problems help make us the people that we are. You might even say that each of us is a diamond in the making.

———

OBJECT FOR SHARING: A diamond ring or earring and a small piece of coal for comparison.

SUGGESTIONS FOR PRESENTATION: If you can find one, wear a hardhat with a light attached such as those used by miners and spelunkers.

FOLLOW-UP ACTIVITIES: Show pictures or a video of how coal and/or diamonds are mined. Lead the children in listing as many uses for diamonds as they can.

A MOUSE IN THE HOUSE

Little things are important too.

"There's a mouse in the house," Mother blurted out to Father. It was a cold winter night and they had just turned out the light.

"A mouse in the house—that simply can't be!" Father cried, tossing in the bed, rubbing his eyes and scratching his head. "I plugged all the mouse holes at the start of last week; I knew they'd be looking for a warm place to sleep. There's no hole for a mouse to crawl through; I've plugged them—that's all."

"But there's a mouse, I tell you. There—did you hear it go *scratch*?"

"Yes, I heard it," Father sleepily moaned, resting on his pillow, soft and warm.

"But you must do something!" Mother shouted and then shook Father from his slumber, cozy and deep. "Go get him now; why, he'll bring his friends. They'll all take over—then there'll be more than ten.

Before you know it, we'll be overrun. There will be mice and more mice, squeaking at our door."

Father threw back the covers and jumped to the floor. "Ouch! It's cold out here!" he cried when his feet touched the boards. Father stumbled down the stairway, following the scratch. He tiptoed all through the house, first this way, then that. Finally, he was able to find the scratch. It came from the fireplace, near the stack of firewood he had split and carried in a few hours earlier to keep the house warm. There on the hearth, in the glow of the fire, crouched a frightened little mouse with his eyes upon Father. *He must have hidden in a hole in the wood*, Father thought to himself. The mouse shook in fright, as though he wanted to say, "Don't put me back in the cold. Please don't send me away."

Father's heart was touched. He didn't know what to do. The mouse had gained his friendship; he was God's creature, too. Just because creatures are little doesn't mean they are not important. Then, in an instant, an idea entered Father's head—a bird cage in the cellar. "That will do nicely," he said to himself.

Father rushed to the cellar and brought back the cage. He lined it with papers and put in some cheese. Father put in some water and set it down by the fire. He pushed the little mouse in and then closed the door. "Good night, Mr. Mouse," Father whispered in glee, then started up the stairs, at last to get some sleep.

"Did you find the mouse?" Mother tugged at his sleeve.

"Yes, I found the mouse," Father said with a smile, as he cuddled his pillow and drifted off to sleep.

OBJECT FOR SHARING: A stuffed mouse.

SUGGESTIONS FOR PRESENTATION: This will make a good pre-Christmas story or a lesson to accompany a special service to bless the animals. Explain how Francis of Assisi loved all animals.

FOLLOW-UP ACTIVITIES: Teach the children about the role that mice and other small animals play in the ecological system. Ask the children to share some stories about the animals in their lives.

THE DIVINE SPARK

Let your light shine.

How many of you like candles? I like candles, too. In fact, almost everyone likes candles. Do you like the smell of this candle? [*Hold the candle around in such a way that all the children can get a whiff of its scent without getting too close.*] Candles are really nice, but we all know that we must be very careful with candles because they can be a real fire hazard and cause things to catch on fire that we don't want burned. You should never light candles alone, but only when adults are around to help you.

I have learned that if I put the lid on this candle, the flame goes out in just a few seconds. Watch. [*Carefully place the lid securely on the candle and wait, as everyone watches, for the flame to die.*] What do you suppose causes the flame to go out when we put the lid on? [*Older children may respond that fire needs air.*] That's right—to burn, fire needs oxygen, just as you and I need oxygen to live. As soon as all the oxygen is burned up inside the jar, the flame goes out.

But you know, this candle has a lot to teach us. Inside every one of you, there is light or a flame that is wanting to burn. Some have called it a "Divine Spark" or a "Spark of the Divine" that we were born with. And the great teacher Jesus said, "You are the light of the world; let your light shine" (Matthew 5:14).

But if we try to cover up the flame or light that is within us, what will happen? It won't burn or shine. At times, others may even think that the flame within us has gone out, just as this candle went out a few minutes ago.

But the difference between children and candles is that the Divine Spark is *always* in there and never completely goes out. It is up to us to uncover the light within us and let it shine.

———

OBJECT FOR SHARING: A scented decorative candle in a jar with a lid, such as one produced by the Yankee Candle Company.

SUGGESTIONS FOR PRESENTATION: Light the candle with a long match from the burning chalice or altar candle at the beginning of the children's message. Many novelty stores sell candles that can only be put out by putting them into a cup of water. Using these could add some humor to your sermon.

47

FOLLOW-UP ACTIVITIES: Explore with the children the practical ways that each one can become "light to the world." A cake decorated with candles might help the children to remember the story of the day.

STAR STUFF

We are all special.

How many of you like to look at stars? There is nothing quite like going out on a clear night where you can get away from artificial lights and gazing up at the stars in the sky.

This time of year, we are reminded of some people of long ago who saw a special star in the sky and followed it in search of a newborn king. Does anyone remember who these people were? That's right—they were called *wise men* or *magi*. They were well-educated astrologers who studied the stars. The story goes that when they saw a new star in the sky, it meant a new king had been born. Christians believe Jesus was the new king who came into the world.

Did you know that you can actually buy a star? There are stars that have not yet been named. If we choose, we can "buy a star" and name it after ourselves or someone else we love.

But if you want to see a star, you need look no further than yourself. Hold up your hand and look at it. You are looking at star stuff. Some scientists tell us that we are made of the same stuff as the stars. Now, what might that mean for us? It means that our lives can shine brightly. It means that we can light up the sky of someone's life by the compassionate and loving way that we live. It means that if we set our minds to it, we can reach and reach and reach for the stars with our hopes, dreams, and plans.

So as we think about the magi and how they followed a star, let us not forget that we are made of the same stuff as the stars. We are "star stuff." And that makes us pretty special.

OBJECT FOR SHARING: A picture of a star (not the star shape), perhaps taken from the Internet.

SUGGESTIONS FOR PRESENTATION: Either the Sunday before or the Sunday after January 6 (Epiphany) would be a good time to present this message. Project a constellation on the ceiling of the worship space.

FOLLOW-UP ACTIVITIES: Encourage the children to study a book of stars or do research on the stars or solar system. If there is one nearby, a visit to a planetarium would be excellent reinforcement.

WHAT MAKES ONE WISE

Seeking the truth is the key to wisdom.

"Father's home! Father's home!" the little boy Sargon cried. He had seen the camels coming in the distance and recognized his father as one of the men in the caravan. When at last his father entered the house, little Sargon was so glad to see him that he leaped into his father's arms.

"Father, where have you been?" little Sargon quizzed him. "You have been gone so long."

"Yes, that I have, Son," replied his father, who was tired and weary but glad to be home. "I have been on a long journey to Bethlehem, a little village in a country far, far away."

"What did you see there, Father?" Sargon asked.

"It was beautiful," the father said, taking his son upon his knee. "I saw a beautiful new baby boy, just like you used to be."

"What was his name?" Sargon asked.

"They called him Jesus," the father replied. "He is a king, and they say he will save his people from their sins."

"But how did you know to go there?" Sargon questioned his father.

"Well, we saw a new star in the sky. And a new star in the sky means a new king is to be born. That's how we knew to go there. We just followed the star until it rested over the place where the baby lay with his mother."

Little Sargon thought about this. Then he said, "Father, is that why they call you a wise man, because you study the stars?"

"Well, I suppose so," his father replied. "But now I think that if I am wise it is for a different reason."

"What reason, Father?"

"I think the person who is wise," the father said, "is the one who goes searching for the truth until he finds it."

"Did you find the truth, Father? Did you?"

"Yes, Son, I think I did. I think I found the truth."

"Can I become a wise man, Father? Can I?" little Sargon pleaded.

"Yes, you can become a wise man, too, if you also go searching for the truth until you find it."

"What is the truth, Father?"

His father smiled, patted him on the head, and said, "I think the truth is called *Jesus*."

OBJECT FOR SHARING: Use a piece of artwork depicting the magi.

SUGGESTIONS FOR PRESENTATION: This story will work best on the Sunday just before or just after Epiphany, January 6, the day the Christian Church celebrates the visit of the magi. Before you begin the story, ask the children if they have ever thought about what the wise men might have said to their families after they returned home from seeing the baby Jesus.

FOLLOW-UP ACTIVITIES: Ask the children to imagine the conversation between the magi and Jesus' parents.

LET MY PEOPLE GO!

God wants all people to be free.

God's people were slaves down in Egypt. And Moses said,

Let my people go!

They had to work hard making bricks for the King. But Moses said,

Let my people go!

And Moses went down to talk to the King. And Moses said,

Let my people go!

But the King of Egypt wouldn't listen to him. "No! No! I won't set your people free." Moses warned the King of the punishment that was sure to come if his stubborn heart didn't change. And Moses said,

Let my people go!

Moses pleaded and pleaded: "Let God's people go where they may worship the Lord." But the King of Egypt said, "No! No!" So Moses said,

Let my people go!

Well, God sent Egypt all kinds of troubles—nasty water, frogs everywhere, gnats all over, flies galore, sores, hailstones, locusts, and darkness. But the King of Egypt was stubborn, so Moses said,

Let my people go!

Finally, finally, when the King of Egypt saw that he could not win, he agreed to let God's people go. But then he changed his mind and started after them with horses and chariots. But Moses said,

Let my people go!

The people crossed the Red Sea and got away from the King's soldiers. When they were safe on the other side, Moses looked across the water at the King and cried "You should have listened to me." And Moses said,

Let my people go!

OBJECT FOR SHARING: A brick to represent the Hebrews' enslavement.

SUGGESTIONS FOR PRESENTATION: Instruct the children to shout "Let my people go!" whenever they hear the cue, "And Moses said." This litany might work well at Passover, when it can be reinforced by the minister or worship committee. Invite the children to stand before the congregation as worship leaders, leading the entire congregation in the response.

FOLLOW-UP ACTIVITIES: Possible topics for discussion might include why peoples are enslaved and how it would feel to be a slave. Upon leaving the sanctuary, the children might work together to prepare a "brick" for baking from mud and chopped straw. You might also invite them to taste salt water, a Jewish Passover symbol of the tears of affliction.

TIFFANY GLASS

We are all valuable.

Perhaps some of you have heard of Tiffany stained glass. Can someone tell us what stained glass is? It is the colored glass that is used to make biblical pictures in many church windows. Mr. Louis Comfort Tiffany started experimenting with stained glass in 1875, and for forty to fifty years his company produced beautiful and very expensive stained-glass artwork from a secret formula—church windows, lamps, vases, and other pieces. Tiny pieces of different-colored glass were bonded together to create beautiful designs.

When Mr. Tiffany died in 1933, the secret formula was lost. No one has ever been able to copy it. Today, Tiffany glass is some of the most valuable stained glass in the world. A small vase or lamp made by Tiffany may sell for thousands of dollars. Every child is like a valuable piece of Tiffany stained glass. When you were made, you were made to be the very best.

But the funny thing about stained glass is that it needs light to shine through it to make it beautiful. Children of the world, like stained glass, come in many different skin colors. Underneath the different skin colors shines the same Spirit who created us. As we let light and love shine through us, we radiate beauty to our world, in the same way that Mr. Tiffany's glass does.

OBJECT FOR SHARING: A picture of a Tiffany window. Or you can point to the stained-glass windows in your church.

SUGGESTIONS FOR PRESENTATION: This story works well near Unity Sunday, celebrated in some churches the third week of January. This is a time set aside to pray for greater religious unity. Project slides of Tiffany windows on the wall so that the entire congregation can enjoy them. Or copy a picture of a Tiffany window onto the front of the worship bulletin using a color photocopier.

FOLLOW-UP ACTIVITIES: Help the children to research Tiffany glass in encyclopedias and perhaps draw and color their own "stained-glass" creations. Use a prism to illustrate how light and colors are dispersed.

WHERE ARE YOU GOING TO SIT?

All people are created equal.

Rosa had worked hard all day long at her job as a seamstress. Can anyone tell us what a seamstress is? That is correct—a seamstress is someone who makes or hems clothes. Rosa's feet and legs were very tired. So one afternoon when she climbed on a city bus to go home, she sat down on the first seat she could find. Since her skin was black, she was supposed to go to the back of the bus, because that is where black folk were expected to sit in those days. But this day, Rosa didn't feel like going to the back of the bus.

Well, when a white man got on the bus, he asked Rosa to get up and go to the back of the bus so he could have her seat. But Rosa didn't want to get up. She was too tired to get up. Besides, Rosa had begun to believe that she was just as good as people whose skin was white and that she should not be punished because her skin was black.

Because Rosa refused to give up her seat in the front of the bus to a white man, all kinds of trouble started. All the black people in Montgomery, Alabama, refused to ride the city buses until the laws were changed to say that black people could sit on the bus anywhere they wanted to. So the buses drove around town just about empty all day for a whole year, which meant the city lost money on its bus system. With the help of a preacher named Dr. Martin Luther King Jr., the laws were changed so that black people had the same rights as white people.

Because Rosa Parks believed that all people are created the same and loved by the Creator the same, the laws in our country started to change, giving equal rights to all people. When she got older, Rosa Parks was awarded the Congressional Gold Medal, a very special award given by the United States government. If you go to Montgomery, Alabama, today, you will find an important street that is called the Rosa Parks Parkway. And it is all because Rosa Parks believed all people are created equal and should have equal respect.

———————

OBJECT FOR SHARING: A picture of the "Freedom Riders" bus and/or Rosa Parks.

SUGGESTIONS FOR PRESENTATION: Before you begin the story, ask the children the following questions: Have you ever ridden on a bus? Where did you sit on the bus? How would you feel if someone told you that you couldn't sit where you wanted on the bus, that you had to go to the very back seat even though other people on the bus could choose where to sit? What would you do?

FOLLOW-UP ACTIVITIES: Ask the children to do research and report back to the group on other civil-rights figures and activities.

GLOVES OR MITTENS

We come to church to be together.

Have you ever thought about the difference between gloves and mittens? In gloves, each of our fingers is separate. Each one has its own little covering. But in mittens, all our fingers stay together in one big covering.

I have learned that my fingers tend to stay warmer in mittens than they do in gloves. Why do you think that is? It is because when fingers are together, the body warmth from each finger helps warm all the others. If they are separate in gloves, then each one is alone and doesn't get the warmth from the others. So when it gets really cold outside, we do better to wear mittens than gloves to keep our fingers warmer.

You know, mittens remind me of the church and how we all come together under one covering. During the week, we may feel separate or alone. The world can sometimes be a cold, lonely place. But then when we come to church on Sunday, we are glad to be with others. We draw spiritual and emotional warmth from each other.

Something else that the mittens teach us is that each of us is important and can share spiritual warmth with everyone else. Each one of us—each one of you—is important and has something good to share with all the rest.

It's good to be together. And each one is important to all the rest. Those are two great lessons we learn from gloves and mittens.

OBJECT FOR SHARING: A glove for one hand and a mitten for the other.

SUGGESTIONS FOR PRESENTATION: This story will be most effective at the coldest time of the year, when children are sensitive to the cold. Before this service, ask each child or family to bring a new pair of gloves or mittens to be donated to a homeless shelter.

FOLLOW-UP ACTIVITIES: Lead the children in collecting the gloves and mittens in baskets or other containers at the close of the story.

THE HERO WITHIN

Anyone can be a hero.

Have any of you ever heard of a boy by the name of Austin Gollaher? Well, if you haven't heard of Austin Gollaher, don't feel bad. Very few people have heard of him. But there is an interesting story about Austin that makes him quite important.

Austin Gollaher was a classmate and friend of Abraham Lincoln, the sixteenth president of the United States. One day, young Abe Lincoln and Austin were playing near Knob Creek, which ran by Abe's boyhood home in Hodgenville, Kentucky. The water was moving really fast because of all the rain that had fallen.

Well, young Abe Lincoln fell into the dangerous stream. He was struggling and fighting the water to make it to the creek bank. Abe very easily could have drowned. What do you think someone might have done to help Abe out of the water? Well, Abe's friend Austin grabbed a long branch that had fallen from a tree and held it out to Abe to grab onto. Austin pulled Abe safely to shore.

If it had not been for Austin Gollaher, Abraham Lincoln might have drowned in Knob Creek. He would not have grown up to become the sixteenth president of the United States. He would not have written the Emancipation Proclamation, which freed the slaves. What a difference Austin Gollaher made for our world by being there to save his friend Abe Lincoln.

I think that we could rightly call Austin Gollaher a hero, don't you? What is a hero? That's right—a hero is anyone who shows great courage and achievement, especially in order to help someone else.

Yet, Austin Gollaher was no different from each of you. Inside each of you is a hero that is just waiting to get out. As each of you grows up, many opportunities will come your way to be a hero. Sometimes it may mean helping other people. Sometimes it may mean standing up for what you know in your heart is right. And sometimes it may mean standing in opposition to something that you know is wrong.

I hope that each of you will see the hero that is inside of you and be that hero whenever life calls upon you to do so.

OBJECT FOR SHARING: A picture of Abraham Lincoln and/or a copy of the Emancipation Proclamation (copied on yellow parchment paper, if possible).

SUGGESTIONS FOR PRESENTATION: This story works well during the month of February, near Presidents' Day. Consider using a long branch to reenact the rescue in the story.

FOLLOW-UP ACTIVITIES: Ask the children what they learned from this story. For instance, we need to be careful about playing around water, and we all need others to be friends to us and help us.

TWO OR THREE IMPORTANT WORDS

It's important to apologize and to forgive.

Billy was the first to arrive at the classroom on Friday morning. The teacher wasn't even there yet. Billy couldn't wait to go to the craft table and look at the ice-cream-stick models his class had been working on before leaving school the day before.

"Wow, that's a nice boat," Billy whispered to himself, as he leaned over the table to get a closer look at Tabitha's model. All at once, Billy lost his balance and fell onto the table, smashing Tabitha's craft to pieces. "Oh no!" Billy cried. "I've ruined Tabitha's boat. She'll be really mad." Billy could hear laughter in the hallway. It was the other students making their way to class. Quickly he took his seat and buried his head in a book.

One by one, the other children came in and took their seats. No one went over to the craft table to look at the models. Billy was glad, because he didn't want anyone to find out what had happened.

At recess, some of the children wandered over to the craft table to admire their projects. Pretty soon, Tabitha came over, too. Immediately, Tabitha screamed, "My boat is broken! Who smashed my boat?" But no one said a word, especially Billy. Maybe if he just acted like he didn't know anything, no one would ever find out that he was the guilty one.

All day long, Billy worried. He couldn't concentrate on his lessons. He felt guilty inside, too, like he should be honest and tell Tabitha it had been an accident. But Billy was afraid, afraid of what Tabitha would do to him and what the teacher would do to him, too.

Finally, the day was over. Billy was relieved. It was time to go home. But all weekend, Billy was unhappy. He knew he had made a mistake and should own up to it, but how could he?

On Monday, Billy could not wait to talk to Tabitha. "Tabitha," Billy slowly began, "I'm sorry. I'm the one who smashed your boat on Friday."

"You what?" Tabitha shouted, coming closer to Billy. But Billy continued, "It was an accident, I promise. I was thinking how nice your boat was when I slipped and fell on the table. I didn't mean to, honest."

For a moment, Tabitha didn't say anything. Finally, she let herself smile and said, "Well, if it was an accident, I guess it's okay. If you really didn't mean to. I guess I can build another one."

"Yeah," Billy agreed, "and I can help you. We'll work on it together." And that's just what Tabitha and Billy did later that afternoon.

OBJECT FOR SHARING: A model of an airplane, cabin, or boat made out of ice cream sticks.

SUGGESTIONS FOR PRESENTATION: This lesson is appropriate for a Sunday when the theme of the worship service is reconciliation, perhaps near the Jewish Day of Atonement. Before beginning the story, ask the children what they think are two of the most difficult words we ever need to say? Three of the most important words?

FOLLOW-UP ACTIVITIES: Teach the children how to make models with ice cream sticks and ask them to work together.

SYMBOL OF HOPE

There is always hope.

I bet some of you recognize the flower I have brought with me this morning. Well, those of you who guessed *daffodil* guessed correctly. A more proper name for the daffodil is *narcissus*.

The daffodil is one of my favorite flowers, partly because it is one of the first to make its appearance at the close of winter and beginning of spring.

I have always admired the daffodil because its roots lie buried in the cold, dark, frozen earth during the long days of winter. And then before the earth has even had a chance to warm up, the daffodil starts coming to life and pushing itself up through the cold, frozen earth until it is standing tall and proud in all its bright yellow glory.

Daffodils can often be seen withstanding the cold February or March winds and even shouldering a blanket of snow.

Because of the daffodil's ability to come up from the dark, frozen earth and withstand cold temperatures and snow and ice, it is a symbol of hope for many.

The daffodil says, "I may be little, but I can be strong! If I can overcome adversity and stand tall and proud, so can you. If I can rise against obstacles to make something beautiful, so can you!"

OBJECT FOR SHARING: A fresh daffodil, or better yet, a bouquet of daffodils, so that you can give one to each child at the end of the lesson.

SUGGESTIONS FOR PRESENTATION: This lesson will work best in late winter or spring, when daffodils are in bloom, perhaps even on Easter Sunday, if Easter falls early enough in the year that daffodils are available. If no daffodils are available, draw one with markers.

FOLLOW-UP ACTIVITIES: Consider putting some cut daffodils in water tinted with food coloring (red, green, or blue) a couple of days before the lesson. This will result in coloring around the edge of the petals. Also consider a lesson on how water makes its way up through the stem and into the petals. Let children draw a small daffodil that they can use as a nametag.

JOHNNY APPLESEED

Spread kindness and generosity.

Good morning, everyone. How many of you like apples? I like apples, too. In fact, fresh apples are good for us.

A long time ago, there lived someone who must have *really* liked apples, because he went all over planting apple seedlings that would grow to become tall apple trees. Does anyone remember the name of the man who planted so many apple trees?

That's right—his name was Johnny Appleseed. Well, that wasn't his real name, the name he was given when he was born. His original name was John Chapman. But people started calling him Johnny Appleseed because he planted so many apple seedlings in the Midwest territory that is now Ohio, Indiana, and Illinois.

As Johnny Appleseed planted apple seeds in the dirt, they sprouted and became seedlings, oh, about this tall. [*With your hands, measure a height of six to eight inches.*] Then he walked over miles and miles, planting the little apple seedlings.

The more apple seedlings that Johnny planted, the more the apple trees multiplied. More trees made more apple seeds, and they were planted and began to grow, too.

You know, you and I may not go about the countryside planting apple seeds, but there is something very important inside every one of us that we can plant everywhere we go. That is the goodness that was placed within us. Not just some of us, but *every one* of us.

And the more we share the goodness that is inside of us—through deeds of love, kindness, forgiveness, and helpfulness—the more that goodness grows, just like all the apple seeds that Johnny Appleseed planted over the countryside.

———————

OBJECT FOR SHARING: A shiny apple.

SUGGESTIONS FOR PRESENTATION: Consider using this lesson in the spring at planting time. Bring a sack with a few apple seeds in it, or secure the services of a second person to walk by with a sack on his or her shoulder. This second person could stoop down a few times as though planting apple seedlings. Or bring a six to eight inch cutting from an apple tree to illustrate what a seedling would look like once planted. You may also want to note that John Chapman was a traveling preacher who spread Universalism as well as apple seeds.

FOLLOW-UP ACTIVITIES: Share apple slices with the children as they return to their seats or go to classes. Consider going on a field trip to an apple orchard to pick apples and then taking the apples to a food pantry or shelter.

BAMBOO MUSIC

Each of us has a beautiful song to share with the world.

Can anyone tell me what *bamboo* is? Bamboo is a tall, slender, woody plant in a grass family that mostly grows in tropical and subtropical areas. Bamboo is often seen growing wild in swampy areas near the sea. Bamboo shoots can be anywhere from 3 feet to 164 feet tall. They can be anywhere from about a half inch thick to twelve inches across at the base. Mature bamboo plants are hollow inside. If we were to see a field of lowly bamboo growing wild, we might think it isn't worth very much.

But you know what? Bamboo plants are among the most widely used plants in the world. It might surprise you to learn that bamboo is used in some parts of the world for constructing houses, rafts to sail on the water, and bridges to cross streams. Bamboo is also used to make wood flooring, baskets, mats to sleep on, hats to provide shade from the sun, fish traps, and even buckets to carry water. Bamboo is also used to make fishing rods, water pipes, and chopsticks. Bamboo pulp is even used to make paper.

But one use for bamboo that is most interesting is for making music. A short piece of bamboo can be drilled with holes at just the right locations to make different notes. [*At this point, either the presenter or someone else in the congregation could play a short piece on the flute.*]

Isn't that beautiful? How much like you and me, I think. Though we may sometimes think of ourselves as little and common, like the lowly bamboo plant, the truth is that inside each of us is something beautiful just waiting to come out. Perhaps it is a song we have to sing. But maybe it is a prayer we have to say, or a kind word we have to share, or a spiritual gift we have to offer the rest of the church community. That thing of beauty may be hidden, but it is there just waiting to be drawn out, as the beautiful music in the lowly bamboo plant is just waiting for someone to come along and blow it out.

OBJECT FOR SHARING: A piece of common bamboo and a flute made from bamboo.

SUGGESTIONS FOR PRESENTATION: As noted in the story, another member of the congregation can stand in his or her place at the designated time and play a short, peaceful melody. The fact that the person does this unexpectedly and from her or his place in the congregation, rather than coming up front, can add to the effectiveness. Try to coordinate this lesson with a service that focuses on music, perhaps specifically music written by members of your own tradition.

FOLLOW-UP ACTIVITIES: If bamboo is available, lead the children in crafting a wind chime from different lengths of bamboo.

PATRICK THE DREAMER

Dreams can change the world.

A long time ago, in a land far, far away, there was a young man who came from a fine family. His father was a deacon in the church, and his grandfather was a priest. One day, while this young man was out walking, Irish pirates kidnapped him and carried him away. He was only sixteen years old. He must have been very frightened as he was tied up and forced aboard a ship and taken to Ireland, where he was sold as a slave. The people who bought him treated him terribly.

One day, this young man managed to run to a boat and escape to France, and then later to Britain. But then something amazing happened. He had a vision, or a dream. And in that dream, the young man was instructed to return to Ireland, where he had been so terribly treated, so that he might tell the people there about God and Jesus. And so he went back to Ireland and he began teaching them the stories in the Bible.

And people listened to him. Before he was finished, he had baptized over 100,000 people into the Christian faith and started over two hundred new churches!

Has anyone guessed who the young man was? That's right—it was St. Patrick, whose birthday we celebrate on the seventeenth of March. Before his death, Patrick was elected Bishop of Ireland.

Patrick's amazing personality, gifts, and love—the same personality, gifts, and love that could be in you and me—enabled him to do wonderful work. He followed his dream and changed the world. And that is why we have St. Patrick's Day.

OBJECT FOR SHARING: A shamrock or three-leafed clover, the symbol of St. Patrick.

SUGGESTIONS FOR PRESENTATION: Do not reveal the identity of Patrick until near the end of the story in order to arouse curiosity and engage the children in guessing who the hero might be. Obviously, this story will work best the Sunday before St. Patrick's Day.

FOLLOW-UP ACTIVITIES: Encourage the children to draw and color a shamrock and to find Ireland on a map or globe. Pictures of Ireland's green landscapes can suggest an interesting correlation to the color green, the color of St. Patrick's Day.

BUMBLEBEES CAN'T FLY

We can sometimes do what seems impossible.

Have you ever thought much about bumblebees? What do you know about bumblebees? One of the things we know about bumblebees is they can sting if we make them angry, especially if we disturb their homes.

But another thing about bumblebees is that they cannot fly. At least, some people say bumblebees cannot fly. Do you have any idea why bumblebees are not supposed to be able to fly? According to some scientific calculations, bumblebees' wings are too small to carry their weight.

But you know what? No one ever told bumblebees that they couldn't fly. So they just do it! In other words, every time we see a bumblebee fly, we are seeing a miracle. We are watching one of earth's creatures do the seemingly impossible.

As we study history, and especially the history of religion, we can read a lot of stories about how people also have done things that seemed impossible. One time when Jesus was teaching, he said that all things are possible for the one who believes (Mark 9:23). Having faith or belief in ourselves and in the power that is within us enables us to do more than we might have ever imagined.

So the next time you hear a bumblebee buzzing around your head, remember that she or he is doing the impossible.

———————

OBJECT FOR SHARING: A photograph of a bumblebee.

SUGGESTIONS FOR PRESENTATION: At the beginning of the story, when children are sharing what they know about bumblebees, encourage them to try buzzing like a bumblebee in unison. Plan to present this lesson in June, when the bumblebee's buzz is a familiar sound.

FOLLOW-UP ACTIVITIES: Ask the children to compile a list of other creatures that seemingly do impossible things. Ants, for instance, carry many times their own body weight. If one is nearby, take the children to visit an insect exhibit at a science museum.

THE RAINY DAY

Look for the good in every situation.

It was pouring down rain when Jake awoke on Monday morning. He dragged himself out of bed and pulled back the curtain of his window to look out at the street. "Drat! I *hate* rainy days," Jake moaned.

When Jake went to the breakfast table, his dad knew that he was unhappy. "What's wrong, Jake? Get up on the wrong side of the bed this morning?" his dad teased.

"It's raining! That's what's wrong," Jake snarled. "I'll get all wet going to school. We won't be able to go outside at recess. And our baseball game this afternoon will be cancelled." Jake played with his breakfast because he was too unhappy to eat.

When the school bus came, Jake ran through the rain and caught it. But he did not like it. He was unhappy all day long. And everyone around him knew it.

That same morning, across the neighborhood, Riley awoke to hear the rain pounding on her roof, too. "Oh boy! A rainy day. I *love* rainy days," Riley exclaimed. Riley hopped out of bed and ran to the window to look outside. She watched the big raindrops splashing on the street. "I can wear my new rain slicker and boots, and I can splash puddles on the way to school," Riley cheered. "If it is still raining when I get home this afternoon, I can curl up in my window seat and read a book while I listen to the rain."

At the breakfast table, Riley was jubilant. "My, someone is happy today," Riley's mother said. "You must have had very pleasant dreams."

"It's raining! That's why I'm happy," Riley smiled. "I *love* rainy days."

Riley couldn't wait to put on her rain slicker and boots. All the way to school, she splashed rain puddles in the streets, and that afternoon, on the way home from school, she splashed them again. After getting an after-school snack, she ran up to her room and curled up on her window seat with a storybook and blanket and listened to the big raindrops go pitter-patter on the windowpane.

———————

OBJECT FOR SHARING: A bright yellow rain slicker, hat, and rubber boots.

SUGGESTIONS FOR PRESENTATION: This lesson will work well in the spring, when we think about April showers bringing May flowers. Before the story, ask the children if things always go the way they want them to. What do the children think is the best thing to do when things don't go as expected?

FOLLOW-UP ACTIVITIES: After the story, ask the children to think about the difference between Jake and Riley. Invite them to share what they like better—sunshine or rain. (Explain to the children that both sunshine and rain are needed to keep life in balance.) For religious educators who are adventurous, letting the children make "mud pies" from dirt and water would surely be a hit.

ROCKY BEAUTY

Beauty is often hidden.

I've often wondered about rocks. Have you? Have you wondered about how rocks were made? How old rocks are? And what a rock's insides looks like?

Some rocks, scientists tell us, were made by volcanoes as they spewed their hot lava high up into the air. Others were made under the oceans as the pressure of earth and water pressed upon minerals and dirt for years and years. Rocks may be thousands, even millions, of years old.

Many rocks appear to be pretty dull on the outside. But if we could see the inside, we might find that those same rocks are quite beautiful, like this one. [*Hold up a geode so that all the children can see inside it.*]

Look how beautiful this rock is on the inside. Fortunately for us, someone knew enough about rocks to imagine the beauty hidden inside this rock and open it so that its beauty could be shared with the world.

You know, we are sort of like rocks. Inside every one of us is a marvelous beauty that was placed within us when we were created. But sometimes that beauty can't be seen—unless we are willing to open ourselves and let it be seen. The beauty we have inside of us is the beauty to create, the beauty to love others, the beauty to smile, and the beauty to laugh and make others laugh.

A rock is a marvelous creation. But so are you!

OBJECT FOR SHARING: A rock that has been cut down the middle so the colors inside may be seen. At specialty gift shops, one can often find bookends created from cut and polished rocks. These will work just as well.

SUGGESTIONS FOR PRESENTATION: If possible, secure a bag of small, colorful polished stones so that you can give one to each child at the close of the lesson.

FOLLOW-UP ACTIVITIES: Take the children on a trip to a museum that has a rock collection. Or someone in the congregation who has an interest in rock collecting might bring in some interesting specimens or even a rock saw to saw rocks collected prior to the lesson.

HEROES WHO HELP HEROES

Each of us can help others to greatness.

I am guessing that at least some of you have heard of Helen Keller. What do you know about Helen? Before she was two years old, Helen became very ill. Her illness left her both *blind* and *deaf*—she couldn't see and she couldn't hear. Try shutting your eyes so that it is dark and then cover your ears with your hands so that you can't hear, and try to imagine for a moment the kind of world that Helen Keller lived in. [*Encourage the children by doing this yourself.*] Okay, you can open your eyes and uncover your ears now.

But even though she couldn't see or hear, Helen learned to read and speak. She was able to graduate from college and became a famous writer and speaker all over the world. Because of what she was able to do, Helen Keller is often thought of as a hero.

But you know what? Helen is not the only hero in this story. She had someone to help her learn to read and write. Does anyone know who that special some-one was? It was another young woman by the name of Anne Sullivan. Anne worked with Helen by letting Helen feel her lips move when she talked and by drawing letters on the palm of Helen's hand. By helping Helen become a hero, Anne Sullivan was a hero herself.

One lesson we learn from the story of Helen Keller and Anne Sullivan is that every one of us has the ability within us to help make others great. We can be heroes by helping others become heroes.

OBJECT FOR SHARING: A picture of Helen Keller and Anne Sullivan.

SUGGESTIONS FOR PRESENTATION: Use this story during a time when the congregation is focusing upon persons with disabilities and the ministry of the church in this regard.

If there is someone available who knows sign language, ask him or her to accompany the presenter and sign the children's sermon for the congregation.

FOLLOW-UP ACTIVITIES: Acquire a book printed in Braille and share it with the children. Discussion might center around public places where they might have seen Braille (public restrooms, motel rooms, train stations, etc.). Teach the children some simple sign language.

THE RIGHT THING

Speak up for what is right.

Roger noticed Larry, Bobby, and Jeremy huddled in the corner when he entered the classroom. They kept glancing over their shoulders to make sure no one was watching. "What are you all doing?" Roger asked, trying to see what they were hiding.

"Shhh!" the three boys replied. "Don't let anyone see. It's Monica's purse. Larry lifted it from her backpack. We're going to divide up the money. We'll let you in if you don't tell."

"Uh, I don't know," Roger replied. He couldn't believe what his friends were doing. They were stealing from one of their own classmates. He knew it was not right. "That's not right!" Roger blurted out. "You shouldn't do it." He turned to walk away. Just as he did, he bumped into their teacher, Ms. Sizemore.

Ms. Sizemore went to the head of the class and asked everyone to take their seats. When everyone had quieted, she said, "Larry, would you please step out into the hall with me?" Larry's face turned red. Slowly he got out of his seat and walked out into the hall with Ms. Sizemore.

In a couple of minutes, Ms. Sizemore stepped back into the room alone. "Bobby," she said, "will you please step out into the hall with me?" Bobby's face, likewise, grew red as he left his seat to join Ms. Sizemore in the hall.

Again Ms. Sizemore stepped back in and called, "Jeremy, will you please step out into the hall with me?" Tears started dripping down Jeremy's face as he slowly walked across the room toward the door. By now, Roger knew exactly what was going on. Ms. Sizemore had caught them with Monica's purse. Now they were being punished.

A third time, Ms. Sizemore stepped back into the room alone and called, "Roger, would you please step out into the hall with me?" Roger was shocked. He had not done anything wrong. But Ms. Sizemore must have thought that he had joined the other boys in taking Monica's purse.

"But, but, Ms. Sizemore, I didn't do—"

Ms. Sizemore put her hand on his shoulder and gently said, "Shhh, Roger. I know you didn't do anything wrong. I heard what you said to the other boys about it not being right. I'm very proud of you, Roger. Within each of us is the ability to do the right thing, and you did. Your parents should be very proud of you. And I am going to make you my special helper today. Come on, let's tell the rest of the class that today you will be the teacher's assistant."

Roger proudly stepped back into the classroom and took his seat. "Class, Roger is going to be my assistant today." A big smile covered Roger's face. He had done the right thing. And it felt good.

OBJECT FOR SHARING: A small purse or wallet.

SUGGESTIONS FOR PRESENTATION: Ask an older child to pantomime or act out the action as you tell the story. This lesson might be planned for a Sunday when reference is made to the Ten Commandments or the inherent worth and dignity of every person.

FOLLOW-UP ACTIVITIES: Lead the children in a discussion as to why it is important to always try to do the right thing and how doing the right thing respects the worth and dignity of others.

THE WHITE PUPPY

On the inside, we are all the same.

How many of you like puppies? [*Ask for a show of hands, but be careful not to let children get off on tangents.*] Well, this morning I have a story about a very special puppy. Once there was a mother dog that had a litter of fuzzy, cuddly puppies. There were six puppies in all. The first few weeks after the puppies were born, they didn't do much but sleep close to their mother and drink their mother's milk.

But after a few weeks, the fuzzy, cuddly puppies began to play in the grass in the warm spring sunshine. One day, one of the puppies began to think about himself, and about his brothers and sisters, and he realized that something was strange. As he watched his five puppy siblings play in the morning sunshine, he noticed that their coats were solid black. Their coats were so shiny and black that they glistened in the sun.

His coat, he couldn't help but notice, was all white. There wasn't a speck of black anywhere on him. Well, this made White Puppy feel funny, and embarrassed, and sad, because he was different from all the rest.

White Puppy lay down by a shade tree on the lawn, and he started to sniffle. Little teardrops formed in the corners of his eyes as he lay and watched the other puppies romp in the grass.

Sensing something was wrong, White Puppy's mother walked over and lay down beside him. "What's wrong, my precious one?" Mother said to White Puppy.

"Mother, why am I different?" White Puppy sobbed. "My brothers and sisters all have beautiful shiny coats of black, and mine is white. What is wrong with me?"

"Oh, my dear, dear White Puppy," the Mother laughed. "There is nothing at all wrong with you. It's just that some puppies are black, and some are white. Some are yellow, and some are red. And others are something in between. That's the way the great Life Maker planned it. We may be a different color on the outside, but on the inside we are all the same.

"Besides, white is beautiful, too, you know. See right here, I have some white on my paw. I've always thought of that little patch of white as being special. And since you are all white, you are even more special to me."

White Puppy's tears had stopped falling, and he didn't feel sad anymore. Giving his mother a loving lick, he jumped up and ran to where the other puppies were playing in the sun.

As White Puppy grew and became an adult, he noticed that, indeed, there were dogs in all shapes and sizes, and there were dogs in all colors, just as his mother had said. And none of them seemed to notice whether one was red or yellow, black or white.

OBJECT FOR SHARING: A picture of a puppy, or if you are really adventurous, a live puppy.

SUGGESTIONS FOR PRESENTATION: Since the story mentions "the warm spring sunshine," this lesson will work well in springtime. Use hand puppets to act out the story.

FOLLOW-UP ACTIVITIES: To help the children make the connection between puppy color and skin color, ask a question such as, "What do you think this story might say to us about the way we see ourselves and others who are different?"

THE CRICKET'S CHIRP

Size isn't everything.

Have you ever taken time to think about the cricket's chirp? Do you know how crickets make the sound that we hear in the late spring and summer? Well, the front wings of the male cricket are grooved or rough. When the male cricket is looking for a mate, he rubs one wing against another, and that is what makes the chirping sound that we hear at night. But the fascinating thing about the cricket is that his tiny chirp can be heard several hundred feet away! It doesn't seem possible, does it? But we all know that it doesn't take something big to make a lot of noise. If you have ever had a cricket in your bedroom at night when you were trying to go to sleep, then you know how loud a cricket's chirp can be.

The important thing to remember is that sometimes little things have great effects on the world around us. Just because we are little doesn't mean we can't do great things.

In Jesus' day, some parents wanted to bring some little children to Jesus so that he might touch them and bless them. Some of the adults who were friends of Jesus tried to stop the parents from bringing their children, thinking that Jesus would not want to be bothered. But Jesus said, "Let the children come to me, and do not stop them. For to them belongs the realm of God" (Mark 10:14). In other words, Jesus was saying that we shouldn't think children are not important just because they're little. Like the cricket, what we do and what we say can have far-reaching effects. So it is important for us to think about how we chirp—how we speak and act.

OBJECT FOR SHARING: A picture of a cricket or a real cricket in a jar or fishbowl.

SUGGESTION FOR PRESENTATION: Play a recording of a cricket's chirp as you are giving the lesson.

FOLLOW-UP ACTIVITIES: If a live cricket is available, lead the children in releasing it outdoors. Follow with a discussion on the importance of crickets in the ecosystem.

Work with the children to compile a list of other small things and how they fit into the order of life.

PEARLS IN THE MAKING

Turn something troubling into something beautiful.

Who can tell us where pearls come from? That's right—pearls come from certain kinds of shellfish, such as oysters, that live in the water. There is an interesting story about how pearls are made.

But first let me ask—have any of you ever gotten sand in your eyes? It is very uncomfortable, isn't it? What do our eyes do when we get sand in them? That's right—they form tears to try to wash the sand out and get rid of it.

Well, some shellfish do something very similar. When certain kinds of shellfish get a grain of sand inside their shells, it is uncomfortable. So these shellfish have been designed to excrete a pearly white substance to cover the grain of sand so it won't be so rough and irritating. Layer upon layer of this substance forms as the shellfish works against the irritant until finally, you guessed it—a beautiful white pearl is made.

You know, it is sort of that way with you and me. We have been created to make something beautiful with our lives. And history has shown that humans created some of the most beautiful things after some kind of trouble or great challenge.

No one has a perfect life free from trouble. But when trouble or disappointment strikes, remember the shellfish, which takes the trouble and turns it into something beautiful.

OBJECT FOR SHARING: A pearl earring, necklace, or other item containing a pearl.

SUGGESTION FOR PRESENTATION: Fasten a loose imitation pearl inside a shell with rubber cement to illustrate where pearls are formed.

FOLLOW-UP ACTIVITIES: Encourage the children to make a list of as many people (such as Helen Keller) as they can think of who responded to life's challenges by making something beautiful for the world.

THE GOLDEN RULE

Respect the worth and dignity of others.

I bet that some of you have heard of the *Golden Rule*. Now, don't say what the Golden Rule is yet, but if you have heard of the Golden Rule, raise your hand. Well, it just so happens that I have brought the Golden Rule with me today. Is this what you think of when you hear someone speak of the Golden Rule? Well, of course not. I am just being a little silly this morning.

If the Golden Rule is not a gold-colored ruler, then what is it? That's right—the Golden Rule is doing to others as you would have others do to you (Luke 6:31). Why do you think it is so important that all of us abide by the Golden Rule? There are many reasons for abiding by the Golden Rule, aren't there? But certainly one good reason for abiding by the Golden Rule is that when we do so, we respect the inherent worth and dignity of others. That is, we respect the value that is in the other person. And we honor the other person as we want to be honored ourselves.

Have you ever stopped to think about the kind of world it would be if no one lived by the Golden Rule? Have you ever thought about all the trouble we would have if everybody did as he or she pleased and didn't care if he or she hurt others? It would be a pretty sad world, wouldn't it?

Most of the major religions of the world teach some form of the Golden Rule. So it must be pretty important. But each one of us is important also. Each one of us deserves to be honored and respected. And that is what we do when we always try to live by the Golden Rule.

OBJECT FOR SHARING: A plastic twelve-inch ruler that has been spray-painted gold.

SUGGESTION FOR PRESENTATION: Spray-paint several inexpensive plastic rulers gold with the words "Treat others as you would like them to treat you" printed and taped to the underside so that you can give one to each child at the close of the lesson.

FOLLOW-UP ACTIVITIES: Lead the children in finding and reading the Golden Rule as it is expressed in different world religions.

WHAT WE'RE HERE FOR

Try to do good whenever you can.

"Mom, what are we here for?" six-year-old Noah asked his mother.

She looked up from the computer keyboard where she was working, somewhat surprised at the question her son had asked. "What are we *here* for?" she repeated the question. "What do you mean?"

"Well, the Rabbi said we should always remember what we are here for," Noah explained. "So I was just wondering—what are we here for?"

Joshua, Noah's older brother, who had just turned ten, had been listening. "We're here to do good whenever we can," Joshua piped in. "God put us here to do good to others."

Again Mom was quite impressed by what she heard. "Tell me more," she invited.

"The Rabbi says that the way we show we believe in God is by doing all the good we can every day that we live. We should try to do at least one good deed every day."

"That's very interesting," the mother said. "And what kinds of things are good deeds?"

Both boys were thinking hard now. Their mother could tell that their minds were working. Finally, Noah said, "How about when we take care of Mr. Goldstein's cat when he goes away to visit his daughter?"

"Yes, that's good, Noah," his mother affirmed.

"And how about when I open doors for people at the synagogue?" Joshua exclaimed.

"Yes, that's good, too, Joshua."

"And when we help our neighbors rake leaves, and take out the trash?"

"And when we give food to the Community Food Drive, and help our teachers straighten up the classroom?"

"Yes, yes, yes, yes!" the mother agreed. "These are all good deeds."

"And that's what we're here for," Noah said.

"Yes—that's what we're here for." Mother looked at her two sons and smiled.

OBJECT FOR SHARING: A religious object bearing the Star of David, the symbol of the Jewish religion.

SUGGESTION FOR PRESENTATION: This story works well when the worship service or

Religious Education class focuses upon some aspect of the Jewish faith, such as the meaning and importance of Passover.

FOLLOW-UP ACTIVITIES: A Jewish prayer cap and/or picture of a Jewish synagogue could serve as good discussion starters after the story. A field trip to a Jewish synagogue, if one is nearby, would be even better.

SUMMER JOURNALS

Everyone has an important story to tell.

Can anyone tell us what a *journal* is? A journal is a book in which someone writes his or her private thoughts. Sometimes it is called a diary. Often, these thoughts are about the person's spiritual life that come during times of meditation, devotions, or prayer. One of the most famous journals that has ever been found is *The Diary of Anne Frank*. This is a journal that a young girl kept during World War II when the Jewish people were being treated so badly. Young Anne wrote in her diary about how her family had to try to hide from their enemies and how hard life was during those years. After the war was over, Anne's diary was found in the house where her family had lived and tried to hide. Because the words she wrote were so powerful, her diary was published so that the whole world could read it. [*The presenter might choose to read a few brief quotations from* The Diary of Anne Frank *at this point.*]

Many great religious leaders have kept journals. One person that comes to mind is Rev. John Wesley, the founder of the Methodist Church. Even though he wrote it over two hundred years ago, many people still study John Wesley's journal today.

Each one of us has an important story to tell. Writing down our important thoughts about our spiritual life helps us to learn who we are and what we believe. As we write down our important thoughts and then go back later and read them, we grow spiritually.

I have brought with me today some small journals in which you might choose to write down your important spiritual thoughts during the summer months. We might even call them our summer journals. If you like, when religious education classes begin again in September, you can bring your summer journals and share some of the things you have written. Perhaps you will enjoy writing in a journal so much that you will find a nice, bigger one at a bookstore.

A key to remember is that your thoughts are important, especially to you and your spiritual growth. And who knows? The words that you write may someday be very meaningful to others in the same way that Anne Frank's words are so meaningful to us today.

OBJECT FOR SHARING: Enough small booklets of folded, lined paper covered with construction paper and perhaps tied in the middle with yarn, with "My Summer Journal" printed on the front cover for every child.

Suggestions for presentation: Bring a real journal or diary to show as an example while presenting the story. Consider sharing a brief quotation or two from *The Diary of Anne Frank* with the children.

Follow-up activities: Encourage the children to put their names on the front of their journals and make an initial entry on the first page during religious education class.

RESOURCES

Anderson, Herbert, and Edward Foley. *Mighty Stories, Dangerous Rituals: Weaving Together the Human and the Divine*. San Francisco: Jossey-Bass, 1998. Discusses the power of religious ritual and myth and how they help us create and express meaning. Shows how ritual and myth connect the human and divine.

Bettelheim, Bruno. *The Uses of Enchantment: The Meaning and Importance of Fairy Tales*. New York: Alfred A. Knopf, 1976. Explores how children's tales can arouse curiosity, stimulate the imagination, and help children discover their self-identity, deal with inner conflicts, and confront their fears and problems.

Cameron, Julia. *The Artist's Way*. New York: G. P. Putnam's Sons, 1992. Cameron seeks, through practical guidance, to bring out the creative energy, what she refers to as "God energy," that is within all of us.

Campbell, Joseph, and Bill Moyers. *The Power of Myth*. New York: Doubleday, 1988. Highlights the power of religious myths, with a focus on the hero that "lurks in each one of us."

Coles, Robert. *The Spiritual Life of Children*. Boston: Houghton Mifflin Company, 1990. Coles gleans a wealth of wisdom from his interviews with hundreds of children from a variety of religious backgrounds. This work reveals the great depth of thought in religious matters that children are capable of when given a chance to express themselves.

Estes, Clarissa Pinkola, ed. *Tales of the Brothers Grimm*. New York: Quality Paperback Book Club, 1999. In her introduction, Estes discusses soul life, innate ideals, and universal thoughts. A good resource for those interested in universal themes and archetypes.

Fahs, Sophia L. *Jesus the Carpenter's Son*. Boston: Beacon Press, 1945. Uses the imagination to fill in the blanks and address the "What ifs" that surround the life of Jesus.

Fahs, Sophia. L. *Today's Children and Yesterday's Heritage*. Boston: Beacon, 1952. Stresses the importance of a child's self-worth, sense of relationship with the larger world, and need to "feel the Mystery of Life."

Groome, Thomas H. *Christian Religious Education*. New York: Harper Collins, 1980. Speaks of the importance of lived faith, becoming what we are called to become, and nurturing human freedom and creativity.

Handford, S.A., tr. *Aesop's Fables*. New York: Penguin, 1994. In the Introduction, Handford discusses the "common-sense and folk wisdom" at the heart of stories and fables.

Harris, Maria. *Fashion Me a People*. Atlanta: John Knox Press, 1989. Notes the importance of spending time alone "in the company of the Divine."

Jordan, Jerry Marshall. *Filling Up the Brown Bag: A Children's Sermon How-To Book*. New York: Pilgrim Press, 1987. Stresses the importance of letting children know they are loved and wanted, nurturing within them an awareness of God, instilling within them a sense of self-worth and a positive self-image, encouraging children to stretch themselves and reach their full potential, and sparking their imaginations.

Rogers, Fred. *Play Time*. Philadelphia: Running Press, 2001. A good resource, most notably for preschoolers, for planning follow-up activities using common household objects. Encourages children's use of imagination and creativity.

Rogers, Fred. *You Are Special*. Philadelphia: Running Press, 2002. A tiny pocket book of timeless wisdom that reinforces the truth that everyone is special. Can easily be worked into many children's sermons.

Wagner, Betty Jane. *Dorothy Heathcote: Drama as a Learning Medium*. Portland, ME: Calendar Islands Publishers, 1999. Though written as a resource for leading children in drama, this is also a good resource—especially the first half—on how to physically present children's sermons. Discusses the discovery of human experience, reaching a deeper insight, and helping children catch a vision of the wider world. Also emphasizes the importance of tapping the energy of the human spirit and valuing human achievement.

ACKNOWLEDGMENTS

I wish to express my deepest appreciation to Dr. Susann Pangerl, director of the Doctor of Ministry Program at Meadville Lombard Theological School; Dr. John Tolley, dean of students and my advisor on this project; and Dr. Neil Gerdes, librarian and third faculty advisor, for the support, encouragement, and guidance they rendered, not only in the course of my doctoral studies in ministry but especially in the completion of this endeavor. I would also like to express my appreciation to Mary Benard, editor at Skinner House Books, with whom it was a joy to work on this project.